OK, LORD, TAKE OVER!

Jesus

As Total Lord

of

Your Total Life

by

George De Prizio, C.S.C.

Dedicated —
> with much affection to
> Bill and Karleen Warnock
> for their inspiration
> and example in
> living the Lordship of Jesus Christ.

PREFACE

In a previous book called, **My God I Need Something**, I have tried to tell my friends in a very simple way what the Christian Renewal in the Holy Spirit is all about. This little book goes a bit further. You see, the work of the Holy Spirit is to lead us deeply into the Lordship of Jesus Christ — to make us cry out with deep faith and childlike joy, "Jesus is Lord!" And saying it sincerely means we try to live with Jesus as total Lord of our total life. This book was written in the hope that under the gentle guidance of the Holy Spirit you will say, "OK, Lord, Take Over!"

My personal thanks to Bruce and Patricia Baker of **CharisMEDIA** who have spent much time with me in preparing the manuscript for the press. And to Bob and Laura Hughes who have continually provided me with a quiet place for writing, hospitality, an office and library, my prayer of thanksgiving, "I thank my Lord for you!"

George DePrizio, C.S.C.

INTRODUCTION

It's a simple fact that many people are making a mess of their lives. You may be one of them. To admit it to others is hard. What good would it do anyway? To admit it to yourself is discouraging. You only feel more frustrated. What good can come of repeating to yourself — I'm a mess?

But you've got to admit it to somebody or else you will burst apart with your uptightedness. Well, there's only one left. That's God.

"Right, Lord," you say. "You are the only One who can understand me. The only One who can help me. Lord, I'm a mess. Take over!"

When you begin to talk that way to God in the person of Jesus Christ you are on your way out of the mess. He takes over in a way that heals you. He rids you of your fears — past, present and future. He gives you new hope, new peace, new direction in your life. How? Well, He invites you to come into His total Lordship. That is, He wants you to make Him total Lord of your total life.

OK, Lord, Take Over!

CONTENTS

Dedication II
Preface III
Introduction IV

Chapter 1 Jesus Christ,
           Lord of Your Past 1
Chapter 2 Jesus Christ,
           Lord of your Present 21
Chapter 3 Jesus Christ,
           Lord of Your Future 30
Chapter 4 Jesus Christ,
           Lord of Your Health 44
Chapter 5 Jesus Christ,
           Lord of Your Treasures 68
Chapter 6 Jesus Christ,
           Lord of Your Heart 86
Chapter 7 Jesus Christ,
           Lord of Your Time 101
Chapter 8 Jesus is Lord! 114

Scripture quotations are from the "Good News for Modern Man," published by the American Bible Society, and are used with permission.

Chapter 1

JESUS CHRIST, LORD OF YOUR PAST

First of all, let's start with your past.

You say, "Sounds crazy. That's what I want to get away from. I'm trying to forget it — the mess I've made of it."

Right you are. You're trying to get away from it because you've made a mess of it. So it haunts you, worries you, right?

"Right. I'd give anything to forget it. I mean the part of it that bothers me, the mistakes and failures and some of the awful things I've done."

You can't forget it. You see, your past is very much a part of you. Everything that's happened in your life right to this very moment. Your memories are all with you good and bad. Whatever you've done, said, thought, and hoped. That past stays with you, for better or worse. Just close your eyes and be quiet for a moment. Suddenly you see yourself down the corridors of your life. Some of them are well-lighted. Some of them very dark. You hear words you spoke — they come echoing back to you through the long years. You relive something that happened to you when you were just a kid. Well, you know how it all sticks to you. And when you least expect it — there it pops up to sting and hurt you.

"I'm with you all the way on that. So what can I do about it?"

You can't do much. You ought to know that by now. Raking over the past can be bad business when you do it alone.

"Are you hinting maybe I should go to a psychiatrist or something like that?"

Sometimes that can help. A psychiatrist can help you in many ways. He can show you why so many things happened to you and what they did to you — how they have influenced your life one way or another. All self-knowledge is good — sometimes very helpful towards peace of mind. But I know many people who have spent hundreds of dollars on counseling and psychiatric help and are right back where they started.

Do you remember the old kindergarten jingle about Humpty-Dumpty? "Humpty dumpty sat on a wall. . . Humpty-Dumpty had a great fall. . . All the king's horses, and all the king's men couldn't put Humpty-Dumpty back together again."

We're all a little bit like Humpty-Dumpty. We've got to be put together again. And very often the doctors and the psychiatrists just can't do it.

"It's discouraging. If I can't do it, and they can't do it. Is there anyone who can?"

Yes, there is ONE who can.

"You mean — God?"

Yes, I mean God in the person of Jesus Christ.

"Well, I've confessed my sins many times if that's what you mean. I've tried — I never get the list right. I don't want to go over all that again."

Thank God for that.

"Why do you say that?"

First of all because your list of sins is only part of your past. There's much more to it than that. Anyhow, your sins do bother you but God isn't looking for your list of sins at all. Do you remember the story of the Prodigal Son?

"Oh — that's like an old chestnut for me. Sooner or later every preacher brings that up. Anyhow, I kind of like it. I suppose it's because I can identify with that prodigal guy myself. But I never get beyond that."

You mean — ?

"I mean I never get beyond the sin part

of it. You know how the son feels about all he's done. But all that about the father — putting the ring on his finger and kissing him and killing the old fatted calf — then having a party. It's a great story. How do I get into it.?"

If you don't mind my pulling that old chestnut out again, let's just go over together what happened. We'll take the main things just as Jesus told them.

> "There was a man who had two sons. The younger one said to him, 'Father, give me now my share of the property.' So the man divided the property between his two sons. After a few days the younger son sold his part of the property and left home with the money. He went to a country far away, where he wasted his money in reckless living. He spent everything he had."
>
> Luke 15, 11-14

You can see that chap had a mind of his own. Strong willed — independent. No one was going to tell him what to do. He knew what he wanted. He wanted to swing a bit. And swing he did. "He wasted his money in reckless living." Talk about your swingers today. Well, you have one there. And sooner or later, like all swingers, he ends up tired, exhausted, drained and penniless. "He spent everything he had." Doesn't that tell the whole story?

"You mean the spending jag means more than wasting money?"

Right. He wasted that and much more than that. His time, his talents — he just made a mess of his life. And he went from one mess to another. When a famine spread over that country he was forced to go to work taking care of pigs. Let's follow the story:

> "Then a severe famine spread over that country and he was left without a thing. So he went to work for one of the citizens of that country, who sent him out to his farm to take care of the pigs. He wished he could fill himself with the bean pods the pigs ate, but no one gave him anything to eat."
>
> Luke 15, 14-17

Now think that over. There's a picture of a human mess. There's loneliness, hunger, and failure. From the big splurge to the pig pen. You know that pig pen is a symbol of how low we can get when we start messing up our lives, doing things our own way. Then we wallow in the mess we ourselves have created.

Anyhow, the story takes a beautiful turn for the better. Just as we see him there in a pretty sad state — even envying the pigs because they have something to eat — he faces up truthfully to the whole sorry fact about himself. And things begin to happen.

> "At last he came to his senses and said, 'All my father's hired workers have more than they can eat, and here I am, about to starve! I will get up and go to my father and say, "Father, I have sinned against God and against you. I am no longer fit to be called your son; treat me as one of your hired workers."' So he got up and started back to his father."
>
> Luke 15, 17-20

Follow this through. There he is in the pig pen. That pig pen is black, dirty and nasty. Deep in that darkness of the mess he has made of his life, he gets an inner light. He follows that light through. "At last he comes to his senses." You see when we are down and out and at our worst, God is always ready to give us the light we need to lead us out of our darkness. That light brings us into what we call — repentance. Do you understand repentance?

"Well, I guess so. Doing penance, you mean?"

That's part of it — but not the first part of it nor the most important. A lot of people spend half their lives making themselves miserable "doing penance" and never get into the real meaning of it.

Try to understand that repentance is first of all not something we do — it's something we think over. The very word says that in its root meaning. You begin to re-think your life. It's something that gets started deep within you. Like the prodigal son you come to your senses. That is to say — you come to your true self.

The prodigal son began to realize what a fool he was — what a mess he had made of his life. So in this re-thinking process he decides to go back to his father. Can't you imagine how he feels when he starts to think about facing his father with his list of sins, and his own words of self-condemnation?

"Sounds like myself the last time I was on my way to make a general confession."

OK, you're in good company then. Or should I say — bad company. Anyhow, listen to what happens now:

> "He was still a long way from home when his father saw him; his heart was filled with pity and he ran, threw his arms around his son, and kissed him."
>
> Luke 15, 21

Well, what do you think of that?

"Wow!"

Wow is right. In a way, that one sentence alone about the father running to greet his lost son and covering him with his love is what the whole Gospel is about. Gospel means good news. If that isn't good news for all of us, what is? I often think how wonderful it would be if that one verse of the Good News could be plastered on billboards all over the country, all over the world. It would make a lot of people aware of who God really is. They'd get rid of the idea of God as the almighty accountant keeping a perfect record of all our sins. People who are a "long way from home," like the prodigal son, would find that once they start to repent — thinking it all over again, God the Father is waiting for them, His heart filled with love and His arms outstretched to hug them.

"It gives me an entirely new idea of God."

Exactly. That's what Jesus wanted to give us through this story. To teach us — God is love. God wants to love and save us, not condemn us. That's why, as the son starts to accuse himself, "Father, I have sinned against God and against you — I am no longer fit to be called your son," the father doesn't pay any attention to him at all. He's simply not interested in that dreary list of sins and all the self-condemnation. Above all he's not going to sit in judgment against his son. He might have said, "I knew you'd make a mess of it and you did it all right." None of that. Instead he calls for a party, a great celebration.

> "But the father called his servants: 'Hurry!' he said. 'Bring the best robe and put it on him. Put a

ring on his finger and shoes on his feet. Then go get the prize calf and kill it, and let us celebrate with a feast! Because this son of mine was dead, but now he is alive; he was lost, but now he has been found.' And so the feasting began."

Luke 15, 22-24

How about that? Doesn't it blow your mind? There he is — the prodigal expecting to be judged, condemned and punished. He had even thought of his own punishment — to be a slave, just one of the hired workers. He would gladly have settled for that. What a surprise when he hears his father calling the servants to clothe him like a prince with the best robe and jewelry. And then a great festival — a celebration in his honor.

Notice how the father orders the prize calf to be killed for the banquet, not just any calf, mind you, but the best, the prize calf. That might seem to you like just another detail. But it says something quite special. It speaks of the overflowing love of the father; his desire to lavish the very best upon his son, to make him feel at home again, loved and wanted. None of that negative, condescending condemning attitude — "Oh, yes, you can come back, but you deserved what you got and I hope you learned your lesson."

Three cheers for the father! That means three cheers for God. Because that's why Jesus told us this story. He wants us to see how tremendous His love is, how ready He is to forgive us. He doesn't want us tortured by the past, memories of sins, failures, humiliation or whatever. Remembrance of past things keeps many people in darkness of spirit. They keep trying over and over to bring their list of sins up to date, to revise it, correct it, confess it all over again. Immersed in scrupulosity, trying to make sure they get everything right, they succeed beautifully in reviving all their guilt feelings. So they live continually in a state of self-condemnation. And living in the state of self-condemnation over the past is a heavy oppression. It causes stress and strain, deprives you of peace of mind and heart, and serves no purpose. It certainly doesn't help you. And it doesn't glorify God. For you do not honor the passion and death of Jesus by wallowing in the mire of the past. He gave every drop of His blood to redeem that past and to reconcile us to His Father.

To make Jesus Christ Lord of your past life is to take the first important step towards inner healing. You yourself can do nothing about the wounds and bruises of your past life caused by your own sinfulness, foolishness, your pride, your anger, lust and sensuality, your greed or envy. You can lament it, strike your breast over it, make lists of sins, keep confessing them, but when you have done with all of this, you are right where you started. Perhaps worse off than ever. You will find the past weighing down on your neck like the albatross bird on the neck of the ancient mariner. The past can be a haunting ghost that sneaks in subtly when we least expect it, that comes in and out. Unwanted and unwelcome it comes, sometimes even in the midst of your joys. No doctor, no psychiatrist can heal you of that past. The only one who can, and wants to, is Jesus Christ.

But you have to release that past to Him in a total and constant surrender. Constant, because as the memories of the past continually come back, in turn you continually assert His Lordship over whatever it is that would drag you down again into self-condemnation, scrupulosity, and depression. "Lord, I leave it all to you.

Lord Jesus, you are the total Lord of my total past life. Take care of it, Lord."

Learn to pray in faith and believe in Jesus as Lord of your past. You will find a healing of your inner spirit in this area, a new peace of mind. When your head starts to ache again with the burden of the past, think of Jesus, the Lord of your past and your Good Sheperd. He will quiet the throbbing and the aching. He is the good Sheperd who makes you lie down in green pastures. He will lead you beside the still waters. He will take your head filled with the irksome noises and voices of the past, and He will anoint you with the soothing oil of His peace and forgiveness.

Aside from our own personal faults and sins, the burden of the past is often made heavier because of wounds and bruises caused in us by the thoughtlessness or even sinfulness of others. Who is there that has not been hurt by someone? These hurts can go way back to childhood. They leave lasting impressions. Often they cut deep within us. And very often they cause resentments. Sometimes we feel them — sometimes we're not much aware of them. But they're there just the same. Do you follow me?

"I do. I know I'm full of resentments. But I can't seem to help it. They keep coming back."

Right. That's exactly the nature of a resentment. It keeps coming back to you. Look at that word "resentment" closely. It will help you to understand what we're talking about. The *re* in front of the word means *again* — like repeat means — say it again, or revise means — go over it again, or retell means — tell it again. Now the middle part of the word is from the Latin which means *to feel* — to experience. So that's what happens when you have a resentment. You feel something negative about someone or something over and over again. It keeps coming back. And resentments can be very deep within you. Sometimes you don't even recognize them but they are there just the same in your deeper self.

"Well, how would that be?"

Let me give you an example. A simple example of how a person can be carrying a resentment deep within him and not really be aware of it, yet somehow it affects his life.

A middle-aged man came to me for help. He was very successful in his work, well-respected in his community. But inside he was all torn up. A bundle of frustrations, fears, inferiority complex. You name it. He had come to a point of crisis in his life. He really wanted to give everything up. You know, like taking a train or plane, and just disappearing somewhere.

Just trying to disappear somewhere wouldn't solve his problem, I told him he would only be taking himself and his problems with him. It came to me very strongly through moments of prayer that he was really the victim of his past. His crisis was bound up with his personal self, the self that reached way back into his childhood. Somehow, I felt that if we could reach into his past, beginning with his earliest years as a child, that it would throw light on what he was suffering now. In other words, I felt that a healing process had to be started inside of him. He was a disturbed man. No peace. No real joy. But a good man, and trying hard, as he said, "to practice his religion."

We prayed a bit for the light of Jesus through the Holy Spirit to bring to his mind anything that might have hurt him deeply, first of all, as a child. Then he began slowly to come up with many things.

For instance, he remembered this:

"I was just a kid — maybe eight or nine. Someone gave me a dollar bill. You know how people will give a kid money and say, 'buy yourself some candy.' I came into the house. My father said to me, 'Where did you get the money?' I told him. He said, 'You are a liar. I won't have a liar in this house.' He was a very strict man. We lived on a farm. On the kitchen wall was a whip. He took it and whipped me. I went to my room and cried half the night."

He said, "I don't know why this comes to my mind."

I said, "I think I know why! Your father hurt you very much. He called you a liar. He whipped you unjustly. You wanted to love your father. Every boy does. Now how could you love him for that? And there's another angle that you must not miss. A father somehow represents God to a child. In that moment, you suffered something deep within you, and you began to resent your father. Somehow you have been carrying that resentment with you all through the years. More than that, just this one little incident has affected your image of God."

He asked, "How do you mean?"

"Well," I said, "maybe without your realizing it you have grown up with the image of a god who is an all-punishing god, the god who looks upon our faults and punishes us. You have been living with the god of authority and punishment. A god who, like your father, sees only the surface, does not really care who you are and how deeply you feel and suffer. Now let me ask you — have you ever forgiven your father for that?"

His answer was what I expected. Simply, "I don't think so."

"Of course you haven't," I said. "A little boy doesn't realize what is happening to him. You did not know what a deep wound had been inflicted in your inner being, that this wound was festering into a resentment against your father. And more than that — this resentment against your father was turning into a resentment against God. You have been carrying all this within you for years. It's been very much a part of you. It's affecting you now, because this wound has never been healed." And of course, he asked me, "What shall I do?"

I said — "It's all done in prayer. Thank the Lord Jesus that this light of the Holy Spirit has been given to you. Ask the Lord for the desire to forgive your father. And forgive him — just as Jesus surely has forgiven him. Ask the Lord to heal the bruise caused by all this, to forgive you for any resentment you have built up against God because of it. This is a very deep and personal prayer. But powerful — because it heals that wound. Or as we say — it heals that memory. And if you ever think of it again, it will not disturb you. You will thank God for his healing mercy. You will have peace, and new light on yourself, your father — and God the Father. It's just an instance of how all things work together unto good for those that love God and are ready to surrender everything in their past life to Him."

Now this is just one instance. As my friend placed himself more and more under the healing light of the Holy Spirit — many other things came to his mind: events of the past — people that somehow had hurt him — and he had never forgiven them.

Persons, incidents, sins, whatever there is of the past, we must learn to make Jesus Christ total Lord of our past. The healing light of His Holy Spirit will pierce through the darkness of yesterday. There need be no haunting memories, no ghosts of yesteryear. Just as Jesus is the light of our yesterdays, so He wants to be the LIGHT of today.

lord jesus,
i thank you for my past
the good days and bad
days of rain with clouds
and the grey all inside of me
sunshine days feeling bright bubbles
oozing out of me.

thank you, lord, my forgiving lord
you haven't looked at my sin list
you have placed a ring on my finger
you have kissed me with your love
and celebrated a feast
in honor of me
your prodigal brother.

lord, you know the bruises and hurts
of yesterday and years past
i've hurt others, lord,
and others have hurt me
and i'm hurting now, lord
hurting hard.

so heal me, lord, forgive me
do a new thing with me
lead me by the still waters
restore my soul
anoint my head with oil
take all the crisscross thoughts
take my bungled and bottled up
memories
clear my mind
and let my cup overflow
with the joy of you
lord of my past!

Chapter 2

JESUS CHRIST, LORD OF YOUR PRESENT

Once you have made Jesus, Lord of your past, you can begin to live today without the fears, and scruples, without any darkness of the past to worry and weaken you. But living TODAY, if it is to be truly a life lived deeply with joy, peace and power, means you must make Jesus, Lord of your present, Lord of your present moment, of the present day.

Today has its succession of moments, hours. Today has its morning, afternoon and evening; its work, problems and play. Living with Jesus Christ as Lord of the present moment, the present hour, living with Him as Lord of the present work or project, the present problem — that's what it amounts to.

Every moment of your life is a great gift of God to you. You can live that moment in your own way, guided only by your own thinking, your own desire. Well, sometimes it works out all right, quite to your own satisfaction. If you are really honest, you must admit you make a mess of that moment.

When you and only you enter into that moment, you bring your weakness, your darkness, your fear, your tension. When you let Jesus Christ enter into it, He brings His life and strength, His light. Living with Jesus as Lord of the present moment makes life strong and exciting. Always full of hope and expectation. It's the one sure and permanent cure for the monotony and routine, the depression of your life.

You cry out, "Lord, how wonderful is the present moment when I live it with you! The drudgery is taken out of it — the burden gone. I can see my life now in a new way, moment by moment as a gift from you. And I proclaim You total Lord of every minute of it."

Jesus said, "I am the Way, the Truth and the Life." Hear this again. Hear it in the present moment. Hear Him telling you He is your way, your truth and your life in this moment, this hour, this day. Are you looking for direction? **He is your way**. Are you searching for light? **He is your truth**. Are you weak and in need of strength? **He is your life**. Hear these words, and find in them a new meaning for yourself. Say to yourself, "Yes, Lord, you want to be total Lord of my total life this very moment and every moment of the day."

If you are like most people, you find that today brings with it a problem, a work to be done, a challenging obligation. Whatever it is, it can worry or distress you if you let it. It can take the joy out of life and prevent you from living the present moment as the Lord wants you to live it. He is the Lord of joy and peace. He never intended your life to be a burden, and if it is a burden for you, chances are you become a burden for others. If you find the burden of the present moment, of today almost too much, perhaps you are insisting on carrying it all yourself. Perhaps you are failing to make Jesus Christ-**Lord** of your burden.

You know he has invited us to make Him Lord of our daily burdens. "Come to me, all you who are weary and find life burdensome, and I will refresh you." (Mt. 11, 28) Is He not inviting you to make Him Lord of your present burden? And as you surrender it to Him, He refreshes you. Surrendering a burden to Jesus is an instantaneous "pick-up." It's great to know that you are not carrying it alone. It's great to know there is someone with you helping to carry all your burdens, who knows what they are, from one end of the day to the other, and who has entered into all the details of every problem of your life. "Cast your care upon the Lord and He will support you; never will He permit the just man to be disturbed." (Ps. 55, 22)

You know the Gospel scene where Jesus has been invited to the home of Martha and Mary. The two sisters are quite different in temperament and attitude. Luke tells us that Mary sat at the Lord's feet and listened to his teaching. But Martha was very busy with all the details of hospitality. She was "distracted with much serving." (Luke, 10, 40 RSV) The sight of Mary sitting quietly at the Lord's feet and listening to Him was a bit too much for her. So she breaks out, "Lord, do you not care that my sister has left me to serve alone?"

You see Martha is very willing to serve the Lord, but she does not yet know what it is to make Him Lord of her service. It is evident that it is all her own work. She is being oppressed and dominated by it. She wants to get everything just right. She is the picture of the perfectionist housewife, dominated by her own efficiency. There's a lot of nervous tension in her. Because she feels she is carrying the burden alone, she becomes critical, even resentful, of Mary.

Now listen to the words of Jesus to Martha: "Martha, Martha, you are anxious and troubled about many things; one thing is needful. Mary has chosen the good portion which shall not be taken away from her." This is not at all what Martha expected to hear from Jesus. Here she is trying to serve Him, and He tells her she is too troubled and too anxious. More than that, He holds up Mary as a better example of what He wants. Mary is quiet and listens to Jesus. She's learning what it is to make Him — Lord of her life.

To be anxious and troubled about our work is to take the joy out of the Now, the present moment. The joy had gone out of Martha's service. In her very efforts to serve the Lord, Martha was making a mess of it. You are bound to mess it up whenever you are anxious and troubled. Jesus is trying to tell Martha there is more to life than increasing its speed, heightening its efficiency. But you do not learn this by allowing yourself to get into a bind over everyting you do, whether it's emptying the garbage pail, working out your income tax or getting to the office on time. You learn it by deciding once and for all to make Jesus Christ Lord of your Today, of the present moment in all its details, sometimes drab, sometimes dramatic. But it's not the details that matter — it's the moment of life that flows through every detail.

Posters are in today. Everywhere we go we see posters, inspirational, comic, religious. If you find yourself distracted by much serving, as Martha was, and don't forget that means torn apart — and when you are torn apart — what good are you? Well, anyhow, if you find yourself distracted by much serving, maybe you'd like to make yourself a poster. Post it on your kitchen wall — or your office bulletin board or in your bedroom. And fill in your name — for Martha is a name for all of us, whether Hattie or Henry, Joe or Judith. Print it in large bold letters. "YOU ARE TOO ANXIOUS AND TOO TROUBLED ABOUT TOO MANY THINGS."

But the whole point of this poster is not to remind you that you are anxious and troubled about many things. It's to remind you that Jesus wants you to take time out to listen to Him, to sit at His feet awhile — that you may make him Lord of your Today. It's only when you make Him Lord of the present moment that you are no longer held in bondage to it. The present moment, the present day has its framework, its limits; but it is fleeting, it's passing. There is something beyond, something greater, and that's really Someone who loves you and cares for you, whose life is your life. That's Jesus Lord of the NOW, Lord of your Present.

Another way to look at it. Live in the charismatic NOW. A charism as you know is a gift. This moment, this day is God's gift to you right now. It can be filled with His life, His truth, His presence. It can be touched with His Joy and Peace. It can be strong with His strength. If you make Him Lord of it!

Or it can be just the other way around. It can be the deadly NOW. An albatross around your neck. A moment to be endured, something you want to get over. "Thank God, it's over with! Thank God this day has gone!" No, God does not want that kind of thanksgiving. He gave you this day, this moment. He wants you to live it, but make Him the Lord of it. Then your thanksgiving will change — and really please Him. "Thank you, Lord, that I had this day, that I lived it with you as Lord of every minute of it."

Try living in the charismatic **now**. You will find a new dynamism, a new excitement to life with Jesus as Lord of your present.

*lord jesus
yesterday is gone
surrendered to you,
lord of my past.*

*Lord, today is here
i'm living it now
this present moment,
your moment, lord,
a gift to me with new life, new hope
new love, new work, new play.*

*how deep it is, lord,
how rich, how holy
when you are
lord of the present.*

*so thanks, lord, for this present moment
and the new one just coming up
thanks, lord, for bringing new meaning
to every moment, every new moment of my
life.*

*lord, you bring yourself
to every moment now
that's why this moment means more
than ever before i knew you
as
lord of my present.*

but now, lord,
the day is filled with you
moment by moment, hour by hour
until tonight when i find you
lord of my rest
every moment of it.

thank you, lord
for today and tonight
for this moment
now and always
thank you,
lord of my present.

Chapter 3

JESUS CHRIST, LORD OF YOUR FUTURE

When you begin to live with Jesus as Lord of today — of your present moment, you will want to know Him as Lord of tomorrow, Lord of your future.

You know that so many of your life's worries and fears are focused upon your future. The thought of what may happen tomorrow can drain you. Will you be in good health? Will you have enough money to pay the bills coming in? Will your oldest boy make the grade at college? Will that alcoholic boyfriend of your daughter straighten out? Well, whatever it is, you are thinking about tomorrow and what might happen.

You know, too, how you think about it. Just to be on the safe side you imagine it happening in the worst way. There is a sneaky fear that clings to you about your tomorrow. It can turn you into a prophet of doom. You get prepared for the worst to happen, in the faint hope that it won't. A spirit of pessimism can take hold of you about your tomorrow so that even if the worst doesn't happen, you are almost disappointed.

Now you may be one of the few who can say — "I'm not really that way at all."

Thank God for that. But let's face it. Most people are worrying about tomorrow. Let's face it, too, that in this country, in a very special way, there is a great shadow cast over your tomorrow by all the communication media, the commercial advertising that wants to fill you with doubt and fear about tomorrow so that you will spend all your money protecting yourself today — against your future.

Are you not told with sure statistics what your chances are that you will need major surgery within the next five years? Are you not told that cancer is lurking, if not within you, at least within one or two members of your family? Are you not told that your bank investment now may soon be worthless — better buy property instead? Are you not told property investment is worthless — better invest in stocks instead? Are you not warned against old age in one of those awful nursing homes? Are you not threatened with sudden death — by plane, auto or simply by crossing the street. So better revise your insurance policies. And the list is endless. The cry is for security, security — tomorrow. Protect yourself against that awful tomorrow. Hurry, hurry. Get new hospital benefits, take on more insurance, plan your old age, spend your evenings groveling in retirement benefits, arrange your funeral. It's later than you think. You cannot begin too soon to worry about tomorrow. In fact, you feel guilty that you didn't begin yesterday to worry about tomorrow. But thank heavens, so you are told, you can start today to defend yourself against tomorrow.

It's sad, isn't it, that tomorrow becomes for many people something like the old story of Damocles, who lived with a sword hanging over his head — poised to fall down upon him when he least expected it.

If your future bothers you even the least bit, watch out. That simple botheration may take hold of you and grow into something deep that disturbs your inner spirit and robs you of the joy of living today. Tomorrow's troubles, tomorrow's finances, tomorrow's illness, tomorrow's retirement, tomorrow's old age, tomorrow's death are destroying many people today. Possibly — you.

There's only one real way out of it. Not

more retirement benefits, better insurance policies, hospital security or what have you. The one real way is always Jesus Christ. Make Him the Lord of your tomorrow.

What does He say about tomorrow? Let's listen:

> "Do not be worried about the food you need to stay alive, or about the clothes you need for your body. Life is much more important than food, and body much more important than clothes."
>
> Luke 12, 22-23

The eating and the drinking and the putting on of clothes is all right. It's part of your life. But your anxiousness about it — that's what Jesus is talking about. His words reveal our selfish fears and worries about tomorrow. Will you have enough to eat tomorrow — to drink? Will you have clothes to put on?

In worrying about tomorrow that way, you are missing the point of life which is more than food; you are missing the point of the wonderful body God has given you which is a temple of that life. Let's keep listening:

> "Look at the birds of the air, that they do not sow, neither do they reap, nor gather into barns; and yet your heavenly Father feeds them. Are you not of more value than they?"
>
> Matthew 6, 26 (RSV)

Have you ever looked at the birds of the air? I mean, really looked at them the way Jesus is talking about? Take a look at them in His way. He sees each bird coming into the eternal plan of God the Father, the plan of creation. In each bird he sees the mystery of life and the Father's desire to sustain that life. And as the Father has created them, the Father's will is to feed them. If you begin to look at birds this way, you will become a fanatic bird watcher! Some of the fantastic love of the Father that feeds even the birds will take hold of you. Then you will understand what Jesus is getting at when he says, "Are you not worth much more than they?"

> "Which of you can live a few more years by worrying about it?"
>
> Luke 12, 25.

Well, what Jesus means in simple, ordinary language is: "Do you think you can add a few more years to your life by worrying about it?" And do you think that all your plans to protect yourself against tomorrow will rid you of your fears of the future. Will not the very plans rise up to worry you? Have you made them right? Are they the very best? Are they foolproof? How long will you live? Is there any doctor, any hospital, any medicine or treatment that can guarantee your life's span?

' "Oh, Lord," you say, "you're right. You and you alone are the Lord of Life. The Lord of all my tomorrows. By worrying about it, I'm foolish. I cannot extend one hour of my life that way. I'm really cutting it off. I know it well — the disease of anxiousness and worry is fatal. It has cut short the lives of many of my friends and relatives. Lord, let those words of Yours keep ringing in my ears until I learn the lesson well. . . ."

"Do you think you can add a few more years to your life by worrying about it?"

> "Look how the wild flowers grow: they do not work or make clothes for themselves. But I tell you that not even Solomon, as rich

as he was, had clothes as beautiful
as one of these flowers."

       Luke 12, 27

There it is now, about the clothing again. The Lord seems to know how much we worry about clothes. We may have a closet full right now, but there's tomorrow's fashions to think about. With prices going up, will we be able to afford that new dress, that leisure suit? What will we look like wearing the same old things? Will your children be dressed as well as the other kids in the neighborhood? Will last year's winter coat last another season?

But take another look at the matter of clothing. It means, too, in a wider sense, everything we think we need in life. It means our selfish panting to be clothed in rigid security. It means our proud desire to say to ourselves and our neighbors: "I have this suit on and I want you to know that tomorrow I'll have another. I know where it's coming from. I have the money. I have made my plans for tomorrow's clothing. I have taken out membership in the 'Prudent Clothing Club — Clothes Guaranteed for you Now, for your Old Age and for Your Grave.' "

You see, our trouble is we don't take time out to watch the birds, to look at the wild flowers. How can we? We are too busy worrying about clothing ourselves tomorrow.

> "It is God who clothes the wild grass — grass that is here today, gone tomorrow, burned up in the oven. Won't He be all the more sure to clothe you? How little faith you have!"
>
> Luke 12, 28

"Right, Lord," you say. "How little faith I have! What you say is so great. It's really what I want to hear — but it's so good that it blows my mind. I suppose that's why I can hardly believe it. But you are the living Word, Lord, the living truth. Help me to believe it. Help me to take time out this very day — to watch a bird, to look at a wild flower in the field. To see the creative hand of the Father in every living thing. Let me feel, Lord, Your own hand touching me, Your voice asking me, "Won't He be all the more sure to clothe you?"

> "So do not start worrying: Where will my food come from? or my

drink? or my clothes? (These are the things the heathen are always concerned about.) Your Father in heaven knows that you need all these things."

Matthew 6, 31-32

Lord Jesus, you are the greatest and clearest teacher. Thanks for your great summary of this lesson: don't worry about where it will all come from, Our Father knows what we need. And Lord, I like that little note about the heathen and their being concerned about all these little things. I can see now why. They don't know You. They haven't heard Your word. But Lord, You have spoken to me now. You have given me this great guarantee, the greatest security so that I don't have to worry about tomorrow, about the future, "Your Father in heaven knows that you need all these things."

> "Instead, be concerned above everything else with His Kingdom and with what He requires, and He will provide you with all these other things. So do not worry about tomorrow; it will have enough worries of its own. There is no need to

add to the troubles each day brings."

Matthew 6, 33-34

Now here is some definite positive direction for your life. Jesus says plainly to be concerned, yes, but about His Kingdom and about what He wants of you. Everything else will be yours in good time as the Father wants you to have it.

Perhaps you are at the point of asking, but what is this concern about His Kingdom? I can't go off to some missionary country to evangelize the heathen or preach a sermon from a pulpit or lead a prayer group. Why you might even say — with seven kids to take care of, what can I do about the Kingdom? Isn't Jesus just a bit idealistic? Or is this just for monks?

Just a minute. Jesus was never unreal. Never impractical. He became our brother and walked with the monks of his day and the drunks and the working girls and the father with seven kids, and the carpenters and the fishermen. You name it. What He's talking about is right down your alley. I might say — it's right in your kitchen with your seven kids, because that's where His Kingdom is. Whenever your concern for those seven kids is with His Faith, His Love, His Service, you are in His Kingdom. And if you are concerned in that way, He will provide you with everything you need, for you are helping to spread His Kingdom right there in your little cottage on Main Street. But if you insist on taking the whole burden of tomorrow on yourself you are simply going to multiply troubles. Jesus is no pious preacher painting a pollyanna picture of life. He knows all about your tomorrow. He knows it will have its struggle, its burden, its problems. But He says: *"Don't worry about it. That's not going to help. Just stay with Me today and I'll help you get through tomorrow. You'll see."*

Now I think you should be able to take all this teaching and pray it out. Let your heart put it all together for you. Your mind won't do it. Your mind wants to see your tomorrow all embalmed in deadly security. Remember one of the key words of Jesus is faith. You can't have your future all wrapped up in health security, retirement security, old age security, financial security, and walk in faith. Faith means leaving Tomorrow to Him. Faith means making Him total Lord of your total future. Not only the rest of this next week — but the days and months and years ahead. It's a great challenge to your faith.

If you make Jesus Lord of your tomorrow — the thought of tomorrow becomes beautiful and even exciting. You lose your gnawing fear. You know that as the clock strikes the hour for tomorrow and a new tomorrow begins, there is Someone waiting for you. Someone who knows your problem, who will help carry your burden because He has been through it all, once upon a time, as He walked the road called Calvary.

Will you try making Jesus Lord of your Tomorrow — Lord of your future? Then maybe your prayer will come out something like this:

lord, i've made you lord of my past
i know it works, i'm no longer bothered by yesterday
lord, i've even quit making general confessions
it's great, lord, to surrender that past to you. . .

and, lord, i'm trying hard to make you lord of today
i know that works, too. . .
today i've had more peace,

*more patience
because of you.
somehow as i tried to reach out to you,
hour by hour.
i felt your love and gave it to others.
when i was weak, i found myself eating of
you
and you strengthened me.*

*now here i am, lord, facing tomorrow.
it feels like a long day coming up, lord,
there's johnny with his trouble at school,
and martha with whooping cough,
and harry's still drinking
and a payment due on the new car
and my mother-in-law threatens to visit,
why does it have to be-tomorrow*

*lord, i've heard you talking about
watching the birds
looking at the grass
just so we can see how your Father loves
us
so much more.*

*lord, i'd like to do that
but there's that report at the office
already past due
i've got to get it done-tomorrow
and lord, i'm due at the doctor's for that*

*check-up-tomorrow
and i'm just a bit afraid he'll ask me to slow down
and who will take care of annie and the kids-tomorrow?
excuse me, lord, there i go, again
i'm a man of little faith
lord, let me hear you loud and clear:
"your father in heaven knows that you need all these things. . ."*

*jesus, take over my tomorrow
be lord of my tomorrow and all my days to come!*

Chapter 4

JESUS CHRIST, YOUR HEALING LORD

Once you have made Jesus, Lord of your past, Lord of your present, and Lord of your future, you are on your way to the reality of the total Lordship of Jesus Christ in your life. Once you say it and mean it — Jesus, be Lord of my life — that's it. But the total Lordship of Jesus has so many dimensions that it is good to get down to a few specifics to make sure you don't exclude any area of your life from His Lordship. The more practical and definite you are, the more you shall experience His love and desire to be Lord in your life.

Let's think about Jesus then as healing Lord. Your health — the state of your health — whether you are sick or well, all this is very much a part of you. It's in your thinking, it influences your actions, your eating, your rest, your recreation. If you are like many people, it may be one of the troublesome areas of your life. The question, "How Are You?" might touch off a whole litany of your aches and pains. And perhaps you don't realize how people might get tired of listening to you. They would rather tell you about their own headaches or heartaches; for health is not only a matter of your body but your whole being — your mental and emotional health as well.

Now when there is a question of your health — let's say something starts to go wrong, you probably think at once of doctors and hospitals, medicines and treatments. Or perhaps you are a "chronic" sufferer. You have had that backache so long, that kidney trouble too long, that blood pressure long enough. Well, whatever it is, you feel like the good woman in the Gospel who had suffered so long and had spent her little fortune on doctors, and there was no one to cure her. Or was there? Let's see what happened to her.

"There was a woman who had suffered terribly from severe bleeding for twelve years, even though she had been treated by many doctors. She had spent all her money, but instead of getting better she got worse all the time. She had heard about Jesus, so she came in the crowd behind him: If I touch just his clothes, she said to herself, I shall get well."

> Mark, 5, 25.

Well, that woman is a well-known character, isn't she? Now it might just as well be a man as a woman. I mean, how many people do you know just like that. They have been suffering for years. They have been treated by many doctors. They have gone to one clinic or another. They end up by spending all their money and not getting any better, only worse. Perhaps it's yourself that's reading this right now. It might be somebody in your family. Or a neighbor of yours right across the street.

Now what makes this woman different is that she had heard about Jesus and she decides He's the One to heal her. Her chances of getting right up to Him are small because of the crowd. But her faith is strong enough to watch for a chance just to touch His clothes. She's heard about Him. She has listened eagerly to the accounts of how He has healed this one and that one. After all, when you have a sickness you keep your ears pretty much open to hear about a doctor or specialist who might be able to help you. Now, this doctor she had heard about was someone without a professional shingle. But somehow He seemed to be able, shingle or no shingle, to take care of such matters as leprosy, lameness, paralysis, epilepsy, blindness, high fevers. And if He could take care of all that, the small matter of a severe bleeding of twelve years would be no problem to Him. It seemed so simple to her now. Why hadn't she thought of it before? Now she knew what she must do, "If I touch just his clothes, I shall get well."

> "She touched his cloak and her bleeding stopped at once; and she had the feeling inside herself that she was cured of her trouble."
> Mark 5, 29

Isn't that something? It really happened. I don't know about you but I can just feel the excitement within her. Inside herself she knew she was cured of her trouble. After twelve years! After so many doctors, so much medicine. So much distress, so much bleeding. Now cured — at last! Alleluias bubbled within her being. But let's get on with it — there is so much more here.

> "At once Jesus knew that power had gone out of Him. So He turned around in the crowd and said, Who touched my clothes?"
>
> Mark 5, 30

Lord, **you say,** *this is just beautiful. You know that Your healing power has gone out of You to cure that woman. Now you want to know who she is.*

You see Jesus reveals Himself always as a personal Lord, a personal healer. There's nothing impersonal, purely professional about Him. He doesn't heal a number in a crowd, an X person, He heals an individual, a human being with a very personal illness who needs a very personal healing. He's always a personal Lord.

> "His disciples answered, You see how the people are crowding you; why do you ask who touched you?"
>
> Mark, 5, 31

And that's exactly what we would have said, Lord, look at the crowd. How can you find who touched you?

"But Jesus kept looking around to see who had done it."

> Mark, 5, 32.

Isn't this something? Jesus insists on looking around. He wants to find her, to speak a personal word to her. The healing has to be total, there remains a finishing touch. He's not content with just stopping the bleeding. There's something more, and it can only be done as she meets Him in a person-to-person encounter. He's not going to let her be lost in the crowd.

> "The woman realized what had happened to her; so she came trembling with fear, fell at his feet and told him the whole truth. Jesus said to her, 'My daughter, your faith has made you well. Go in peace, and be healed from your trouble.'"
>
> Mark 5, 32-34.

There it is. This woman, this beautiful person, comes trembling to His feet. Well, who wouldn't tremble a bit? There's a great humility and simplicity about her. She realizes that something wonderful has happened to her. But maybe she shouldn't have touched Him. Maybe she should have asked for permission. Did she do the wrong thing? Maybe, since she had sneaked behind him to touch his clothes and had taken advantage of the crowd hiding her, maybe He didn't want to heal her at all. Did she get a healing by fraud? Anyhow she falls at His feet and admits what she's done.

I can just hear her say, "Lord, I just had to do it. Twelve years of bleeding, Lord. No doctor to cure me. No more money left to look for more doctors. I knew if I could just touch You, You would take care of me."

It's a beautiful moment as Jesus congradulates her for her faith, confirms the healing, and gives her the assurance of His healing Lordship in her life.

And she didn't have to pay a cent. . .

If you've followed this through, you might say perhaps, that's just one of those gospel stories. Yes, just one but if you really read the life of Jesus in the gospels of Matthew, Mark, Luke and John, you will be kept busy checking off all the people that He went about healing! The paralyzed man, the official's daughter, the two blind men, the ten lepers, the dumb man. You will find individual accounts of personal healings like the one we just shared together. Every now and then you will find a great summary of His healing ministry. For instance:

"Jesus went all over Galilee, teaching in their synagogues, preaching the Good News of the Kingdom, and healing people from every kind of disease and sickness. The news about Him spread through the whole country of Syria, so that people brought Him all those who were sick with all kinds of diseases, and afflicted with all sorts of troubles: people with demons, and epileptics and paralytics — Jesus healed them all."
Matthew 4, 23-24

And if you are thinking merely in terms of "just gospel stories," not really true, then you'd have to give up believing in Jesus and believing in the Gospel. Most of the Gospel is about Jesus healing people in one way or another. The Good News of the Kingdom is that God is with us in the person of Jesus healing His sick children.

The Good News is — Jesus is Healing Lord!

But your difficulty, if you have one, is the difficulty of most people. And that is, not that they don't believe that Jesus healed all these people from diseases and sickness; the difficulty is believing that Jesus, right here and now, can and wants to heal you.

Maybe you're saying, "That's right. That's my difficulty, that's right where I am."

You don't stand alone on that. I see now that most people readily accept Jesus as Saviour and Redeemer. I see many that get into His Lordship to the point of making Him Lord of their past, present and future. But I find too few who are willing to accept him and recognize Him in faith as personal Healing Lord.

You might ask, "Well, what does this mean anyway? Aren't we supposed to go to doctors? Are hospitals out? Do we throw away our medicine cabinets?"

I didn't say that. But I have to admit now that in the lives of many people whom I know personally, who have discovered Jesus as healing Lord, that it comes to that — or almost.

But ordinarily you don't throw away your medicine, and cross the doctors and nurses off your list. All these are part of the healing plan and the healing power of Jesus.

Then you come right back and say, "So what are you talking about?"

I'll tell you if you can stand one man's testimony:

"A little over five years ago I was a sick man. Nothing in particular, mind you. But I was beginning to feel the aches and pains of middle age. And I began to take my aches and pains to doctors. Doctors prescribed medicines. Medicines piled up in my cabinet. And some of the aches and pains went away and were soon replaced by others. And some got worse and I continued to look for better doctors and more effective medicines. I began to feel that I was 'over the hill now' and that I must be sick if not most of the time, at least part of the time. What's a middle aged man without a backache, a bit of high blood pressure, an attack of kidney trouble now and then, a few asthmatic evenings.

"In the meantime I began to feel low. No one realized it but I suffered from much depression. There was the thought of really serious sickness coming, the thought of getting old. Anyhow I started to carry the whole package around with me. This is it, I thought. This is the way it has to be. And everybody else I talked to was pretty much the same way. 'How's your arthritis? What's your blood pressure today? John has asked for a week off — I guess the old heart isn't pumping right anymore.' You know, sickness talk. Common misery, common cold. Sons of Adam — have to suffer. Vale of tears. Grin and bear it. Who said life is just a bowl of cherries? It's just a sick go-round of one darn thing after another. Stick to your Blue Cross. Get your White Cross. And don't forget Ever-Ready Ambulance Service.

"Yes, that was my life. Until I heard about people receiving the Baptism of the Holy Spirit and coming into a new kind of life 'in the Spirit,' and how it changed their lives. And since living in my body was no joke, I thought living in the Spirit might do it. More out of curiosity than anything else I went to one of those prayer meetings everybody was talking about. I felt it wouldn't do any harm. As a matter of fact, Church bored me. But I wanted to hang on to God somehow. You know, better be on the safe side.

"Well, you won't believe this. But I got into those prayer meetings and started to like them. And one night the thing they called Baptism of the Holy Spirit happened to me. It really did. And I just felt like a new man. A new meaning to my life-because for the first time I found myself talking to Jesus Christ like a real person talks to another real person. You know, He just came into my life. But the aches and pains were still there, though I felt much better — not so depressed anyhow.

"Then I heard this preacher talk about Jesus as Healing Lord. I had never thought of Him that way. I never thought He'd be interested in an old hypochondriac like me. He's got troubles enough, I used to say — with the Pope and the Bishops and the way they're trying to run the Church, and with all the Protestants coming in (I'm a Catholic). Anyhow, why would Jesus Christ be wasting His time on my backache?

"Well, this preacher convinced me through his own testimony. He said, 'Every morning when I wake up, I proclaim Jesus Christ as total Lord of my total life. Then I say, "Jesus, you are my personal healing Lord. Give me this day all the health, strength, energy I need to really live my life, to do the work You want me to do this day. Let the healing light of Your Holy Spirit lift me in moments of depression or weariness — Lord, baptize me with Your own healing strength.'

"And this preacher said anytime during the day he felt any ache or pain he turned to His healing Lord. 'Lord, just take care of this, Lord, I know You want me well.'

"Anyhow, he claimed that day by day he had all the health and strength he needed. He didn't worry about the next day. Just one day at a time. Little by little, he said, his medicine cabinet had fewer bottles and tubes in it. He hadn't seen a doctor for several years.

"Well, it made sense to me. Why not! This Baptism of the Holy Spirit made Jesus very real to me. And being that real, I said, Lord, you can heal me, too. Let some of Your healing power flow through me. I'm tired of being sick and tired, of being a sick man. I'd rather live in health for Your glory.

"You know, it works! Yes, it works. The old back-aches are gone. Most of my medicine is gone. I get special prayers for healing sometimes when I'm at my prayer meetings. But most of the time I'm just praying to my healing Lord."

To discover Jesus as healing Lord is not only to enter into the healing of your whole being, it is also to find a new way of life, a new attitude, an attitude that radiates health and energy and strength instead of weakness and illness. You see, for many people sickness is a habit they get into. Once they have experienced illness, they get accustomed to it as a normal condition of life. Since they are in the habit of sickness themselves, they take it for granted that everybody else must be sick or at least should be, because that's the way it is.

Recently, a man who came to me for counseling gave me an itemized list of all his bodily troubles. It was like a chapter from an encyclopedia of anatomy and diseases of the human system. When he reached his last gasp, he said to me, "And what do you have? Surely you must have something!"

Lifelong members of the Spirit of Sickness Club like to feed upon others for sympathy. More than that they like to proselytize. Come and join our Club. Get into the swing of one or two diseases and we'll make you a life-long member.

There are instances in the Gospel of what we may call the spirit of sickness or infirmity. Here's one about the crippled woman that Jesus healed on the Sabbath:

> "One Sabbath day Jesus was teaching in a synagogue. A woman was there who had an evil spirit in her that had kept her sick for eighteen years; she was bent over and could not straighten up at all. When Jesus saw her, He called out to her, 'Woman, you are free from your sickness!' He placed His hands on her and at once she straightened herself up and praised God."
>
> Luke 13, 10-13

Don't be shocked at that expression "an evil spirit." Other translations read "she was possessed by a spirit of infirmity" or a "spirit that drained her strength." One of the definitions of evil is anything which causes pain or trouble. Now this is what we are talking about. It's the mental habit in many people of thinking themselves habitually ill. If you ask them, "How is your health?" you may expect the reply either expressed or implied, "I have none." In other words, they have accepted the spirit of illness into their total being. That spirit, that mental attitude surely drains one's strength, or whatever one has left of it; it is bad, it is injurious to the total personality and in that sense it is certainly evil.

If you are interested in reading the full account of this woman whom Jesus healed on the Sabbath, you will find that Jesus says that Satan had kept her in bondage for eighteen years. Well, no doubt there is a power of darkness that can keep people in bondage of illness. We won't go into that here. We don't want to begin thinking that everyone that is sick for a long time is in the bondage of Satan. But what we are getting at is the habit of thinking of oneself as a sick person; that is the beginning of darkness within us. It cannot be of the Lord, for Jesus is always healing Lord. He has given us His Holy Spirit to be our healing light to overcome all darkness within us.

I think Jesus as Healing Lord had a great compassion for those who have given up the hope of ever being well again. Do you remember the man at the pool of Bethzatha? That pool had something special about it. Every now and then an angel of the Lord went down into the pool and stirred up the water. And the first person to go into the pool after the water was stirred up was healed, cured of his sickness or whatever he had. Now let's get to the man who was healed directly by Jesus.

> "A man was there who had been sick for thirty-eight years. Jesus saw him lying there, and He knew that the man had been sick for such a long time; so He said to him, "Do you want to get well?"
> John 5, 5-6

Jesus knew the man had been sick for such a long time! He could see into that long time suffering, the days, months and years, the living half-alive, the weariness of it all. And he could also see the faint hope in the heart of this man that someday he might be the first to get into the pool after the stirring up of the water.

Why does Jesus ask him, "Do you want to get well?" I don't know. But I don't think it was just a casual question. You see, people who have been sick for a long time give up once and for all the idea of healthy living and often don't want to get well. The first step towards healing is simply to want to get well. Anyhow, the sick man answers:

> "Sir, I don't have anyone here to put me in the pool when the water is stirred up; while I am trying to get in, somebody else gets there first."
>
> John, 5, 7

At this point, whatever hope the sick man had of getting healed was a very faint one. He doesn't even answer Jesus' question. He just admits defeat. He's quite accustomed now to being just as he is — a sick man. No use wondering about getting well or not getting well.

If you read on, you know this has a happy ending. Jesus healed him. It must have come as quite a shock to this man. He had long ago given up thinking of himself as a person in good health, as somebody who could walk normally, and go back to work. His hanging around the pool had become such a habit with him. He had the comfort of others around there, some worse off than he was. It was fun once in a while to see who would get into the pool first. Maybe he joined the others in cheering as the lucky person healed came up from the pool. Did he join in placing bets on who would be first the next time to get into the pool for a healing? Anyhow, he never thought of anything ever happening to himself that might make him well again.

You see there are an awful lot of people paralyzed in life by some sort of sickness — hanging around their own pool of Bethzatha. It might be a hospital, a clinic, a nursing home, their own bedroom, or their living room rocking chair. And they are lamenting the fact that there is no one to help them. They have tried all the doctors and all the medicines.

Actually, at this point, there is no one to help them unless they are ready to meet Someone who has a special compassion for long-time sufferers, for people with a spirit of infirmity. He is always ready to ask the question, "Do you want to get well?" Only sometimes they are not always ready to hear that question because they really don't want to get well. In that case, Jesus as Healing Lord cannot act.

But when a person really wants to get well and claims Jesus as healing Lord, something is bound to happen. You see, Jesus heals today — just as he did in the past through the power of the Holy Spirit. A sick person who claims the strength and health of Jesus through the healing light of the Holy Spirit begins to mobilize all the recuperative and life-giving forces within him. God will not use us as puppets. WE have to do something — to reach out, to claim his healing power, to desire to be healed. Discovering and claiming Jesus as healing Lord means the spirit of sickness leaves us. Even though the bodily infirmity may stay on, we are cleansed of our inner darkness that clings to illness and causes much mental depression.

The first healing is always within us. In the Latin language the word to heal is *sanare*. Our English word *sane* derives from this word. Jesus as healing Lord restores us to sanity. A sick person — a person who holds fast to the habit of illness, shrivels up within himself; we may say he is slightly insane, off balance, really not normal. Jesus gives us back our life balance as the spirit of illness is flushed out of us by the energizing power of His Holy Spirit. Once that happens, it is amazing how often bodily and organic ailments are cured. You know by now that most of your ills come from within. And when the within part of you is cleansed, the bodily part of you begins to function better.

To discover and claim Jesus as Healing Lord is to come into what I call a "baptism of healing." He baptizes us with His own healing power and strength through the action of His Holy spirit within us. We begin to think healing, speak healing, act in a healing way. We are delivered from the bondage of a spirit of infirmity. And this gift of Jesus as Healing Lord to us becomes in turn a great gift to others. We no longer focus upon illness in others, speaking about it and giving them false and conventional expressions of sympathy. "Oh, you poor dear, I know what you're suffering. . . my Aunt Hattie suffered from the same thing. And she died from it." As we have claimed the baptism of healing from Jesus our healing Lord, we become a force of healing for others. God can begin to use us as healing instruments in a special way.

If you have received this word and it makes sense to you, begin to act upon it. Even now, ask the Holy Spirit to lead you into the healing Lordship of Jesus Christ. The role of the Holy Spirit is to lead you into the deepest reality of the life of Jesus and a great part of the reality of Jesus is that he is Healing Lord. Pray your own prayer to your Healing Lord — to Him who wants to heal you, make you "sane," restore you to balance. Maybe you will want to start with something like this:

lord, jesus,
you are my lord, i want no other
you are my saviour, my redeemer, my very brother
and thank you, lord, for you are my
baptizer in the holy spirit.

lord, i've thought of you often in all these beautiful ways
but i never thought of you
as my personal healing lord

but now i know better.
now i know you want to be total lord of my total life
that means not only surrendering to you
it means receiving from you
your health and your strength
through the healing power of your holy spirit.

*lord, i'm sick
and so often sick and tired
and my aches and pains come and go
fears, too, because i'm afraid of illness.*

*lord, jesus, be my healing lord!
take the sickness habit out of me
deliver me as you delivered the crippled woman
and the lame man*

*deliver me from thinking of myself as sick
deliver me from all fear of disease
let me come into your own healing strength
through the energizing power of your holy spirit.*

*use me, lord, to bring your healing strength to others
not to cast disease upon them with my foolish words
are you sick? you look so bad —
but to bring them to you as healing lord
for you are jesus christ,
the same yesterday
today
and forever*

*and as you healed yesterday
when you walked this earth
healing the blind and the lame
the woman with the twelve year
hemorrhage
and even peter's mother-in-law
and the ten lepers and all the rest —
you heal today.*

*you want to heal me now, this very day
and every day of my life
even tomorrow, yes tomorrow
for you are jesus christ
yesterday and today and tomorrow
the same forever*

*and i'll not fear sickness
past, present or future
for you are jesus christ
my healing lord.*

Chapter 5

JESUS CHRIST, LORD OF YOUR TREASURES

If you are faithfully following the light that leads you into the total Lordship of Jesus, you will soon find He wants you to make Him Lord of ALL YOUR TREASURES.

You say, "Well, what's what? I don't have any treasures."

Oh yes, you do. I mean the things you own. You may not own much. You may be like the hermit in his bare cell with only bell, book and candle. But those are his treasures. Even that cell is his treasure. Whatever it is, great or small, of value or of no value, it is part of your life and you've to decide who will really be Lord of it — you or Jesus Christ.

"You mean — I have to give everything up?"

I didn't say that. You need your house and your car and I don't know whatever else you have. But now you have to decide who really owns it — who is the real Lord of it — you or Jesus Christ.

"Does it make any difference?"

It makes a great deal of difference. If you decide you own it, it has your stamp and seal on it. You begin to treasure it. You begin to feel you wouldn't know what to do without it. And it's quite possible that as your ownership desire grows stronger and stronger, it begins to possess you. You end up by being owned by the very thing you cling to. You are no longer a free man. You are in bondage to your own treasures. You begin to worry about them. So you take out higher insurance. And the ownership of one little treasure leads to the love of owning another.

"I begin to get it now. But it worries me. If I can't own what I have and it's not right for me to want to have more, it just messes everything up."

Now you haven't understood me. First of all, you say it worries you. Let's see about it. So many fail to come into the total Lordship of Jesus Christ because they think he's out to do them in — to take things away from them, to deprive them of what they've worked hard to get, to reduce them to poverty, or whatever.

That's not the point. Jesus Christ came to free us — to bring us into the full freedom of the children of God. He came to free the captive. So many are held captive by the things they own and by the desire they have to keep on owning. A very poor man in his own way can be held captive by the few miserable objects in his little shack — just as much as a rich man can be a slave to his limousine, yacht and mansion. A great saint once said, "What does it matter if you are held down to earth by a string or a rope? You are still held down."

Jesus Christ doesn't want us held down — in captivity to anyone, and still less to anything. To make Jesus Lord of all we have and need is to come into great freedom of spirit. It brings much relief. We are no longer held captive by anything — whether a pin or a nail. a mansion or a bungalow, a factory we own or a carpenter shop.

If you want to make Jesus Lord of your treasures, you will need the light of the Holy Spirit to guide you through the living Word of the Gospel. First of all, you need a new mentality, a new way of thinking about material things. If you have been clinging to things for most of your life — and building your castles in Spain thinking of a larger home, a bigger car, a swimming pool off a larger patio, this will not be easy.

Your deep desire — deep in you, to possess and own more things and better things will rebel against it. You've simply got to see this through the light of the Holy Spirit, otherwise you can't do it. Rules and formulas won't do it. It's not a question of how much you give to God, let us say by tithing, and how much you can keep for yourself. I have known good people who felt obliged to tithe, practically forced into it by the stirring word of some enthusiastic preacher, and then little by little gave up doing it. You cannot proclaim Jesus Lord of your treasures, you cannot tithe, you cannot give to the poor and share your possessions, unless you have the light of the Holy Spirit to lead you, and the faith and love that His light inspires.

A millionaire friend of mine who felt depressed because he was being accused of being one of those "filthy capitalists who don't do enough for the hungry and the poor of the world" said to me, "Will somebody please tell me what I'm supposed to do? I have a foundation for charitable works. My name is on a dozen buildings that I've given — hospitals, college buildings. What am I supposed to do? Is it wrong for me to have several homes and all the things I've worked for?"

This is a good man and he was sincerely depressed. Yet, following a Christian way of life for many years by trying to fulfill Church obligations, he had not come into the full light of the Gospel. His material possessions — all the six beautiful homes, and the stables, and the dog kennels had started to oppress him. Was he supposed to give them up? How could he?

And you know you just can't tell a man like that, "Why you have to give up some of those things. You have too much. Many people in this world have too little. Some are homeless; you have six mansions. Some are hungry and thirsty; your dinner every night is a banquet and your daily snacks alone would keep a family in food for a week."

All of this is true. But telling him what he should do isn't going to give him the power to do it. "Where your heart is there is your treasure." Jesus said it. If your heart has been with industry and high finance and luxury living, a moral sermon on giving a good part of it away isn't going to to it. And if he does give some of it away so that a few more people are fed and clothed, the effects of this will not be lasting. Didn't Paul hit it hard when he said, "I may give away everything I have, and even give up my body to be burned — but if I have not love, it does me no good." 1 Cor., 13, 3

There are an awful lot of people who are clinging to their possessions like mad, and who put a little salve on their bruised consciences by filling baskets of hand-me-down clothing for the poor and making out an occasional check for "personal charities" (always making sure of the income tax deduction — and after all, if we don't give some of it away, the government will get it). That kind of giving really doesn't help to solve the problem of the world. And the problem of the world is hatred, injustice, oppression, exploitation, greed. The problem of the world is "nothing succeeds like success." The problem of the world is the pride of life, the pride of money and fine furnishings and fancy clothes. The problem of the world is the scorn of the poor, and the respectable tolerance and condescension towards them. After all, says the good Christian, didn't the Lord say, "the poor you will always have with you. . . " Why all the excitement about the have-nots. Let those who have enjoy it, and those who have not, try to get along.

And many good people fail to come into

the total Lordship of Jesus Christ because they have not been courageous enough to open their hearts to Him, afraid this means opening their pocketbooks and their bank accounts as well. They have not yearned for the deeper light of the Spirit and the baptism of love so that the hungry and thirsty brother and the naked child and the man in cell block number 22 become Jesus Christ hungry and thirsty, Jesus Christ naked, Jesus Christ in prison. "I was hungry and you gave me to eat. . .I was thirsty and you gave me to drink. . .I was naked and you clothed me. . ." You see, it is love of Jesus and love of your neighbor because of Jesus — that must be at the root of all the giving, if you have it to give. Otherwise, you will not be helping to change the world. You will simply be dealing with conscience money.

Jesus said:

"No servant can be the slave of two masters; he will hate one and love the other; he will be loyal to one and despise the other. You cannot serve both God and money."

Luke, 16, 13

Perhaps you remember this preached in a sermon by your priest or minister. Very likely you heard him use another translation, "You cannot serve both God and mammon." Now that word *mammon* actually gets to the point better than just saying money. You see Mammon is the false god of riches and avarice. When we say *mammon,* we think of riches almost as an object of worship: wealth as an evil, not because it is in itself evil, but because it easily robs us of our love of God, and it subtly steals our heart away from Him who alone is our true treasure. Our God is a jealous God. He created us out of His eternal love that we might know His love and the true riches of His presence forever. He hates a divided heart.

The tragedy of many good people is trying to serve God with a divided heart. They certainly don't want to give God up, but they don't want to give up anything else either. So they end up midway between God and mammon. They never enter into the fullness of peace and joy promised by Jesus himself. You cannot really be filled with His peace and joy if at the same time you are trying to fill your house, fill your bank account, fill your wine cellar. The peace and joy promised by Jesus is for those who enter fully into His Kingdom, not one foot out and one foot in. That's why he said:

> "How hard it is for rich people to enter the Kingdom of God! It is much harder for a rich man to enter the Kingdom of God than for a camel to go through the eye of a needle."
>
> Luke 18, 24-25

If you understand this right, you know that Jesus is not condemning once and for all, riches and rich people. But he says it's hard for rich people to come close to God and have the joy and peace of His Kingdom, His abiding presence. After all, when you are living it up quite happily in the Kingdom of Gold, chances are you don't want to be bothered too much with the Kingdom of God. In fact, you might not want to be disturbed by it or think about it at all. For that Kingdom belongs to the poor —

> "Happy are you poor; the Kingdom
>   of God
> is yours!

Happy are you who are hungry
   now;
you will be filled!"

      Luke 6, 20-21a

To be concerned about the Kingdom of God is to be concerned with the poor and the hungry. First, with our hearts, because we love them; then with our pocketbooks, if we are in a position to help them. But if our concern is only for mammon, be it small petty mammon, or large luxurious mammon, then we cannot stand firmly with two feet in His Kingdom. If we do not learn what it is to make Him Lord of our treasures, we may have to face an awful condemnation:

"But how terrible for you who are
   rich now;
You have had your easy life!
How terrible for you who are full
   now;
You will go hungry!"

      Luke 6, 24-25.

Do I hear you say — "Thank heavens then, I have no easy life and my bank account is even now overdrawn. I told you I don't have much."

But can you say, "Lord, I thank you that I don't have much. And Lord, what I do have, I make you Lord of it."

You see, it isn't first of all what you have or what you don't have, but your attitude towards it, and whether or not you make Jesus Lord of it. Many a poor man is greedy and living in avaricious desire to be rich, and living with his heart full of hatred and resentment towards the rich. Jesus wasn't speaking of him at all then when He said:

"Happy are you poor; the Kingdom of God is yours!"

You see, he's not really poor though he may have no more than a pot of beans. What Jesus was talking about, points first of all to the way we think about our treasures, the place we give them in our lives and the way we love. If I have a loaf of bread, am I ready and willing in love to share it with my brother who doesn't have even a crumb? And if I don't have any bread at all, am I still thankful and hopeful that God will provide for me — or am I resentful and jealous of those who do have it?

You really can't make Jesus Lord of all you have — Lord of your treasures, unless first of all your mind gets into His thinking, and your heart gets into His loving. It means a radical change in your thinking, and a radical way of love. A radical way of thinking because you own a house and suddenly you can say — "Lord, YOU own it!" A radical way of love because it opens your heart to your neighbor in need — whether he lives across the street or lying naked on some street corner in Bombay. Your excessive love of things may often keep you from loving the one who most needs your help. Yet these things are passing and perishable, whereas love endures. As the poet Patrick Kirby writes:

> "I have loved many things;
> too many things I have loved
> That are forever gone,
> That are forever going. . . ."

In the parable of the rich fool, you will find the mind of Jesus on this whole question of riches, and your treasure-whether it is great or small. Just listen:

> "A man in the crowd said to Him, 'Teacher, tell my brother to divide with me the property our father left us.'"
>
> Luke 12, 13

Here's a man very much concerned about property. He and his brother just can't agree. Evidently, there has been some family wrangling about what belongs to me and what belongs to you. It's the old, old story. The division of property is creating a division among the brothers. This man evidently thought Jesus had the answer and the authority. However it may be, we know he had been listening to Jesus and found his teaching good. "This man is fair, this man is just, I'll ask him to put in a good word for me and order my brother to divide that property." That was the thinking that very likely prompted him to go to Jesus for help.

> "Jesus answered him, 'Man who gave me the right to judge, or to divide the property between you two?' And he went on to say to them all, 'Watch out, and guard yourselves from all kinds of greed; because a man's true life is not made up of the things he owns, no matter how rich he may be.'"
> Luke 12, 14-15

How do you like that? You might say, "quite a switch, and the man worried about his property rights must have been flabbergasted." Jesus tells him point blank, he has not come to be a real estate lawyer, a judge over property problems. He hasn't come for that at all. Then he makes clear why he has come — to point out in what a man's true life does consist. And that true life is not found in the things he owns, no matter who he may be, a retired Palm Beach millionaire, or a bulging oil man from Texas. You simply cannot find your true life in money or the things money will buy. So watch out — in your little hut, you can get just as greedy over a dollar as the millionaire in his mansion over the next big deal.

Jesus had turned away from the man to the crowd. The whole crowd needed to hear this. The man and his brother were not the only ones. Everybody has some kind of money problem, property problem, ownership problem — even though the only things he has are the clothes on his back. And if the only things you own are the clothes on your back, the money problem and the ownership problem may be inside of you because of your greed or your desire to have more, to keep up with the latest fashion, or the new trend in suburbia. That is why Jesus told the man and the whole crowd this parable:

> "A rich man had land which bore good crops. He began to think to himself, 'I don't have a place to keep all my crops. What can I do? This is what I will do,' he told himself; 'I will tear my barns down and build bigger ones, where I will store the grain and all my other goods. Then I will say to myself, Lucky man! You have all the good things you need for many years. Take life easy, eat, drink, and enjoy yourself!'"
>
> Luke 12, 16-19

Let's stop right here so we can get to know this rich man who really has it made. He's rich, and his big problem now is to find a place to store his over-abundant crops. He's got barns, oh plenty of them. They look kind of small to him now. Why not tear them down and build something really big. Then he'll be all set for life. As he builds the barns in his own mind, the thought of that easy life, *"la dolce vita,"* just sweeps over him. Hallelujah for bigger crops, bigger barns and bigger living! Now let's go on with the parable.

> "But God said to him, 'You fool! this very night you will have to give up your life; then who will get all these things you have kept for yourself?'"
>
> Luke 12, 20

And Jesus concluded:

> "This is how it is with those who pile up riches for themselves but are not rich in God's sight."
>
> Luke 12, 21

There goes *la dolce vita* — the easy life, the eating and the drinking, and the bigger crops in the bigger barns. You know, if you look at it in a very human way, you almost rebel against it. Remember the poet who said, "Thou hast conquered, oh pale Galilean and the world has grown cold with thy breath"? Here is Jesus, the pale Galilean taking the easy life with all its riches for a ride, telling us it leads nowhere, it means nothing. Piling up riches for oneself is foolishness, selfishness. It does cast cold breath over the heaped up banquet table and the marble mansion, doesn't it? And the luxurious yacht seems to sink under the weight of His words and even the polo grounds seem less exciting. It's hard, yes, but that's the way it is. HE said it.

But is it really hard? Not when Jesus is Lord of your treasures. Whatever you have or own now or in the future is under His Lordship. You are not like the man who kept everything for himself. You will know how to own and use whatever you have. You will know how much to keep — how much to give away. Whether you keep or give away, it will all be done in love for His glory. Your treasures will no longer possess you. You have turned them over to Jesus, Lord of your treasures.

lord jesus,
you said — where your heart is there is your treasure
lord, i want my heart to be with you
take all my treasures
take my little two bedroom house,
my mansion with parquet floors
take my bicycle, motorcycle,
my cadillac car

take my piano, kettle drums
my spanish guitar

take my paintings
rubens, utrillo, toulouse lautrec
take my rowboat, sailboat, my dream of a yacht
take my double knits and levis, my ties by cardin,
my pants suits and jewelry, dresses by lanvin

my six wigs for evening, my slippers for noon,
my perfumes and roses
and that old silver spoon

yes, lord, you know the list
you know all that i own
it's yours lord, for keeps
all i ask, lord, is a loan
a permanent loan of your love and your light
to guide me aright
in the matter of treasure.

all i ask is none but you, lord
lord of my heart and lord of my home!

Chapter 6

JESUS CHRIST, LORD OF YOUR HEART

To make Jesus Lord of your heart means He becomes Lord of your love. Everyone knows the heart is the symbol of love. Through the ages all men of all races and cultures have recognized and understood love always with the heart as the expression of that love. Even the little child knows this. "Daddy, Mummy, I love you with all my heart."

And God the Father knows this. He knew it from all eternity as he looked upon the Heart of His only Son; the Heart that would be big enough to contain the whole world — all the men and women and children, all the saints and the sinners. The Father knew the love of Jesus would be the expression of His own eternal love. And Jesus knows this, for He came into our world to bring us the love of the Father so that everyone might know that God is love. He died of heartbreak on the Cross for "having loved His own He loved them unto the end. . . . " And the Holy Spirit knows this, for His great work is in the depths of the human heart — to melt it, transform it and pour into it the love of Jesus.

But there's another side of the story. Just as the heart can be a fountain of love as God intends it, man can make it a cesspool of darkness through the little seed of rebellion in him that is always trying to take God's love out of us. You see when love goes out of us, we are no longer in His Kingdom. His Kingdom is love. And Jesus is the Lord of love.

Do you remember the time when the Pharisees and teachers of the Law came to Jesus to complain because his followers didn't wash their hands in the proper way before they began to eat? You will find it all in the 15th Chapter of Matthew's Gospel. Anyhow, there's Peter and all the rest of these men who followed Jesus sitting down to eat without giving a hoot about the point by point etiquette of washing one's hands. And the Pharisees and Teachers were stewing in their righteous britches over it. After all, they worshipped the God of perfect propriety, and they just couldn't stand it. They asked Jesus, "Why is it that Your disciples disobey the teaching handed down by our ancestors?"

And Jesus, with a little trace of Irish in

His Jewish ancestry, answers their question by asking them one, "And why do you disobey God's command and follow your own teaching?"

Then He lets them have it. He tells them they are way off the track in the way they distort God's command to honor father and mother. They twist that command around to suit themselves. Then comes the punch line:

> "You hypocrites! How right Isaiah was when he prophesied about you!
>
> "these people, says God, honor me with their words, but their heart is really far away from me."
> Matthew 15, 7, 8.

Where was their heart? Not with the God of love certainly. But with their own way of thinking, of judging, of condemning. They lashed against the disciples of Jesus for not washing their hands before eating. That meant the food they ate was unclean. And that was against the law to eat unclean food.

But Jesus said to the crowd — *they're all wrong. They're teaching man-made commandments as though they were God's rules.* And He called the crowd to Him and said to them:

> "Listen, and understand! It is not what goes into a person's mouth that makes him unclean; rather, what comes out of it makes him unclean."
>
> Matthew 15, 10-11.

Well, does this blow up a storm. The Pharisees were quite hurt by what Jesus said. The disciples tell Jesus about it. And if I may say so, He just didn't bat an eyelash. *Just don't worry about them, they're blind leaders. And you know what happens when the blind lead the blind — everyone ends up in a ditch.*

It's about time for Peter to get into the act and he does. He wants to know what this all means. Jesus speaks very bluntly to him and the crowd. *You're not any more intelligent than the others. Don't you understand?*

> "Anything that goes into a person's mouth goes into his stomach and then on out of the body. But the

things that come out of the mouth come from the heart; such things make a man unclean. For from his heart come the evil ideas which lead him to kill, commit adultery, and do other immoral things; to rob, lie and slander others. These are the things that make a man unclean. But to eat without washing your hands as they say you should — this does not make a man unclean."

Matthew 15, 17-20.

Now I hope you're getting the point we made before. That is, the heart can be a fountain of love. It can also become a cesspool of all the worst things you can think of. And it all goes back to the heart. Because all the worst things we do or say or think are all failures in love. Failure to love God — failure to love wife or husband, child or relative, friend or enemy.

That is why, if you want to make Jesus Lord of your heart, the first thing is to clean it out. If I may say so, you may need to flush out all the bitterness, all the resentful feelings, the tendency in you to judge and criticize, to back-bite and condemn. If there is the least bit of hatred or feeling against anyone, how can you expect to make Jesus-Lord of your heart? He does not reign over discord, an unforgiving spirit, a streak of vengeance. He can't; that's not His place. That's the kingdom of darkness and you know who reigns over that. He can't be Lord of your heart if you exclude anyone, anyone at all from it. Maybe somebody who has what you think is the wrong color has never really come into your heart. Then forget about Jesus as Lord of your heart, because you should know the Lord is color blind. Just doesn't see white or black, yellow or red — all He sees are children of the one Father. And if those people across the track who don't wash their hands before eating have never nestled in your heart, then forget about Jesus as Lord of your heart. He loves them. They're His kind of people. He sat and ate with them, and he didn't wash His hands before eating.

Then there's your in-laws. Where have they been all these years since you married Horace or Edna? Just floating around on the fringe of your heart? Fringe benefits of your marriage, but not really part of your heart. Then forget about Jesus as Lord of your heart. He loves in-laws. Don't forget, He even healed Peter's mother-in-law.

But what about the Protestants, if you are a Catholic. Where have they been all your life? Outside of you, in the no-man's land of heresy and schism, and you can't really get too close because they have the odor of excommunication about them? And until your Church disinfects them with the proper disinfectant, well really, how can you open your heart to them. Then forget about Jesus as Lord of your heart. He loves the Protestants. He died for them, too. He said, "If anyone loves me He will keep my commandments, and my Father and I will love him and we will come to Him and make our dwelling with him..." And He knows there's many a Protestant brother keeping his commandment of love, even though he can't understand holy water.

And what about the Catholics, if you are a Protestant. Where have they been all your life? Oh, you do know one or two that you can stand, but they're exceptions. Didn't your grandmother warn you. . . "beware of those Catholics, they're wolves in Roman clothing. . .whatever you do, don't marry one, and if you do, I'll disown you. . ." Well, forget about Jesus as Lord of your heart. He isn't the One you think He is. He's not just the Lord of the Protestants. Because when he died on that Cross there were no Protestants to reign over, and for several centuries after that he didn't know a single Protestant. As a matter of fact, he doesn't know Protestants or Catholics or Methodists or Baptists, and Episcopalians, or whoever you are thinking of. He just knows and carries in His great heart all of us, just all of us.

And you might ask — "You mean, even the Jews?"

And I might say, oh my dear, even the Jews, and above all the Jews. Because let me whisper it to you, dear, Jesus was a Jew and His mother Mary was a Jew, and all that gang that followed Him were Jews. And did you ever know a real Jew who was unfaithful to His own?

"You just mentioned Mary. She doesn't fit into my heart. I've always been afraid of Mary. Our preacher once said — she's a Catholic heresy."

Then forget about Jesus as Lord of your heart. Because if there is anyone first in the heart of Jesus, after His Father, it's Mary. What kind of Son would he be not to love His own Mother? And if Jesus loves His Mother, how can you leave her out of your heart? It's your fear of "something Catholic" creeping in. Perfect love casts out fear. Try to hear Jesus saying, *"If you love Me, you'll take Me as I am, with My Mother and My Jewish Brothers and my Catholic and Protestant friends, and My white and black and red and yellow relatives. I am Who I am, I am God's love to the whole world. No exception. No way, no way at all.*

Well, if you're getting the point, you know now, that to make Jesus truly Lord of your heart is to open your own heart to just about everybody you can think of — and then some. You see, just as there is no limit to His love, there can be no limit to yours.

But you ask, "How does this happen anyway?"

You just make up your mind that it has to happen. Let it happen. But you can't do it. He can do it for you — if you will let Him. Jesus didn't give us the law of love just to make it impossible for us to love that way. If we're not loving that way, it's because we've never really wanted to, or we have never tried, or simply because we have never asked for the baptism of love.

"Now wait a minute. Just how many kinds of baptism are there anyway? I know baptism of water and I know now the baptism of the Holy Spirit. Then you spoke of the baptism of healing. Here you throw the baptism of love at me."

Now don't get excited. It's a way of expressing the yearning of your heart to love the way Jesus wants you to love. It's a desire for His compassionate love. It's wanting to be immersed in love. It's knowing in practice what Jesus means when He says, "By this all men will know that you are my disciples, if you have love for one another. . ."

It means you live with the words of Jesus ringing in your ears. "Love one another, just as I love you." It's also a fear that you might be keeping someone outside of your heart — no matter who.

It's so great, you can't do it by yourself. That kind of love has to be poured into you by the Holy Spirit of Jesus. The fruit of the Spirit is love and Paul says:

> "God has poured out His love into our hearts by means of the Holy Spirit, who is God's gift to us."
> Romans, 5, 5.

You see, there's an awful lot of love in you that you have never poured out to others. And when we don't pour it out, God's love dries up within us. St. John tells us the real proof that we truly love God is found in our love for our brothers and sisters.

Now it's only the Holy Spirit who can melt our hearts, and cleanse them of every last trace of coldness, indifference, resentment, hard feelings, grudges and all the rest of the human package. When you are ready to make Jesus Lord of your heart, be sure He is always ready to take over. And He takes over by enkindling within you the fire of His own love through His Holy Spirit.

Many people come into a more abundant Christian life through the Baptism of the Holy Spirit. But sooner or later they backslide. The reason is they have never made Jesus Lord of Love, Lord of their hearts. Our prayer groups are often filled with people who are strong in prophecy, beautiful in praising God in tongues, effective in a healing ministry, and yet limited and weak in their love.

If you want to make Jesus Lord of your heart, take another look at one of the greatest teachings on love ever given by man. That was a man who once hated, once persecuted the Christians. That was a man who could get upset because people didn't wash their hands the right way before eating. Yet that was the man who later said:

"I pray that you may have your roots and foundations in love, so that you, together with all God's people, may have the power to understand how broad and long and high and deep is Christ's love. Yes, may you come to know His love — although it can never be fully known — and be so completely filled with the perfect fullness of God."

The man who wrote that is Paul, the great lover of Jesus Christ, and because he loved Jesus Christ he could love Jew or Gentile, rich or poor, learned or ignorant. This is the man who could say:

"Keep on loving one another as brothers in Christ. Remember to welcome strangers in your homes. There were some who did it and welcomed angels without knowing it. Remember those in prison, — as though you were in prison with them. Remember those who are suffering, as though you were suffering as they are."

Hebrews 13, 1-3.

Because he lived the Lordship of Jesus Christ and knew the love of Jesus, Paul could write his hymn of love. It could only have been inspired by the love of Jesus as the Holy Spirit poured that love into his great heart.

"i may be able to speak the languages of men and even of angels,
but if i have not love,
my speech is no more than a noisy gong or a clanging bell.
i may have the gift of inspired preaching;
i may have all knowledge and understand all secrets;
i may have all the faith needed to move mountains —
but if i have not love,
i am nothing.

*"i may give away everything i have,
and even give up my body to be burned
but if i have not love,
it does me no good.
love is patient and kind;
love is not jealous or conceited or proud;
love is not ill mannered, or selfish, or
irritable;
love is not happy with evil,
but is happy with the truth.
love never gives up;
its faith, hope and patience never fail.*

*"love is eternal
there are inspired messages,
but they are temporary;
there are gifts of speaking in strange
tongues,
but they will cease;
there is knowledge but it will pass.
for our gifts of knowledge and of inspired
messages are only partial;
but when what is perfect comes;
then what is partial will disappear.*

*"when i was a child,
my speech, feelings and thinking were all those of a child;
now that i am a man,
i have no more use for childish ways.
what we see now is like the dim image in a mirror;
then we shall see face to face.
what i know is only partial;
then it will be complete,
as complete as god's knowledge of me.*

*"meanwhile these three remain:
faith, hope and love;
and the greatest of these is* **LOVE**"

1 Cor. 1-13.

Chapter 7

JESUS CHRIST, LORD OF YOUR TIME

The take-over by Jesus becomes complete when there is no area, no dimension of your life where He does not rule by His love.

For instance, He becomes Lord of your time. Time is His gift to you, every moment of it has a meaning and purpose. How do you use it?

If you are honest, you will say like so many others, "Sometimes I use it well, sometimes I half use it, sometimes I waste it."

I think one of the saddest expressions on earth is, "What a waste of time!" But sadder than the expression is the reality of the waste. I hear people say, "I wasted two hours watching television . . .I wasted my money and time on that silly movie . . .I wasted the whole afternoon . . .I wasted the weekend." Yes, what a waste of time!

And wasted time involves waste of God's grace and blessings, waste of talent, waste of money, waste of rest and recreation, waste of love and service, waste of growth in life in the Spirit.

The waste of time we are talking about means we are not using it the way Jesus wants us to use it. You can have a high-powered efficient executive who works into the night, when he should be sleeping, who thinks the only purpose in life is increasing its speed. He is the man of whom people will say at his wake, "Poor fellow! He worked himself to death." Or perhaps you may know the perfectionist housekeeper who just has to keep cooking and scrubbing and polishing and washing all the day long. And some of this, too, is a waste of time. Because sooner or later, time must be taken out for sickness and hospital, and treatment for mental and emotional stress.

It was never the plan of God that man should misuse his time — either by too much work or too little of it. You can misuse your time just as an alcoholic can misuse a vintage bottle of burgundy, or a gourmet can turn a meal into gluttony. The burgundy is a gift of the Lord, and the food we eat is also his gift. Both can be used or misused. Every moment of time is His gift to us. You can use it one way or the other for your blessing or condemnation, for joy or misery.

Making Jesus Lord of your time makes

all the difference. You discover so many things you really hadn't thought about before. For instance, you soon learn that your Lord is more the Lord of rest and play than He is of work. You know He has not destined you for work forever. No one has ever talked about work in heaven! He wants you to take your rest. He is the Lord who has told you to take time out to watch the birds and look at the flowers of the field. He is the One who has spoken to you over and over again:

> "Come to me you who labor and are overworked, And I will refresh you."
>
> Matthew 11, 29.

He is the One who knew what it was to get away from the crowd, to be quiet, to go off in a boat alone, to walk by the lakeside. He's not the Lord of the assembly line and high speed human engines. He's not the Lord of overtime work, when it exhausts you and leaves you drained. He would rather have a sink piled high with dishes waiting to be washed than a fretful, nervous housewife. He cannot be the Lord of the VIP who lives in his office and neglects loving his wife and children.

And facing another side of the time picture, He cannot be Lord of those who let the moments dribble away bored to death because they can't find anything to do. He cannot rule over time spent in silly or sinful pleasure. He knows your need for a refreshing drink and a few minutes conversation with your best friend. But He's gone when you start worshipping at the altar of Bacchus on some bar stool until midnight.

Let's face it. Jesus was often accused of going out for supper and of wining and dining with His friends. But He was never wasting His time. Every moment of His life, He was where the Father wanted Him to be and for a good reason. He spent His time in a way that perfectly accomplished the Will of His Father. Sometimes, it was preaching the Good News, sometimes, healing the sick. Much of His time was in direct prayer with His Father. Much of His time He was alone with His disciples, teaching them and praying with them. But He took time out to talk with the woman at the well; He took time out to shed tears at the grave of Lazarus — He didn't hurry the resurrection of Lazarus. He took time out to have supper with His disciples before he went on to Calvary. On the way of the Cross He took time to speak to the women of Jerusalem who mourned His suffering. And on the very Cross in the agony of His great suffering, He took time to speak to Dismas — to assure him of paradise.

Even as a boy, He knew the great meaning of time. He skipped off from his parents to be "about His Father's business." And He always took time to celebrate the various feast days. One of His greatest celebration times was when He got on a donkey, and rode slowly into Jerusalem listening to the alleluias and the hosannas of the crowd.

He knew when things must be speeded up. He could say — you have to make friends quickly with your accuser on the way to court, and don't let the sun set on your anger. He could say to Judas, what you have in mind to do, do quickly. But He could slow people down, as when He told Martha to take a look at Mary and take things a little easier. In fact, I think Jesus would have loved our everyday expression, "Take it easy." He didn't come, you see, to make life hard for us. But to teach you how to take it easy, even in the busy routine of your life.

Making Jesus Lord of your time brings your whole life into balance and under quiet, serene control. The rush and the nervous tension, the hurry to get things done and the frustration when you don't get them done — all that goes out of your life. It's another phase of your total healing and a beautiful one because it goes on every minute of the day.

You say, "If I give Jesus all of my time, I won't have any left for myself. You know, the things I want to do, when I want to do them..."

First of all, get it right. It's not a question of giving Jesus all of your time. It's yours and He doesn't want to take it away from you. But He wants you to make Him Lord of all your time here on this earth. And when you do that, you'll find you have plenty of time for yourself.

Time involves many things. For instance, time involves your talents, the development of your personality. Every minute of the day you are growing, maturing, learning, creating. Or you are stopping, stunting yourself, taking steps backwards rather than forward. So many have lost control of their time and live an abortive life. They lose touch with the creative powers within them; they fail to develop their talents.

With Jesus as Lord of our time, we begin to use it well, and we fear to waste even a minute of it. The result is we have time to do many things we have always wanted to do. It's a tragedy that so few people do anything about developing the talents and gifts God has placed in them. Those talents and tendencies to want to do this or that are placed in you for a purpose. They are a part of you — and the better part of you will come out as you take time to work out your talents and improve them.

I know a butcher who has made Jesus Lord of his time. He has a busy day at his meat shop, yes. He's tired when he gets home, yes. But he has a little talent for painting pictures and he finds time to work at it. He knows he will never be a great painter. That's not his aim. His aim is to make good use of his spare time. "I used to waste a lot of time," he tells his friends. "I'd get impatient around the house, tired of watching TV, growling at my wife. Now Jesus is Lord of my life and Lord of my time. Funny when that happened, the Lord seemed to say — get out your paint brushes. . ." Developing his talent for painting has made him a more interesting person and a better butcher. He's more composed and calm when he's cutting up a side of beef. Painting even comes into his conversation. "How's that for a saddle of lamb — doesn't that make a beautiful picture?"

Many a father of a family has some talent or another. It might be cabinet carpentry, or poetry, or playing the violin, or sculpture. Or maybe it's an interest in stamp collecting or craftsmanship with toothpicks, or growing roses. If he doesn't take time to get into it and do something with it, he not only fails himself — he fails his children. He fails to give them the inspiration and example of his own creativity, to kindle within them the desire to use their imagination, to be creative and develop thier own talents.

What we have said for the father of a family goes for the mother of a family. How boring for the children when they see mother only as the one who gets their breakfast, packs them off to school, does the dishes and the laundry. She has never taken time out to read a few lines of poetry that she herself wrote, to reveal her yen for ballet, to design flower arrangements — so that Johnny or Janie will say proudly, "Mummy, did you do that?"

You see, when Jesus becomes Lord of our time, then you will discover that you have time to do these things, to develop your talents. You will learn that whatever light there is in you is not given to be kept hidden under a bushel, but to be brought out and placed where your family, your friends, your fellow workers can see it. Somebody needs that light. It isn't just for you alone.

A man once confided to me, "As a boy I lived in poverty. My father was an immigrant laborer — he dug ditches and cleaned cesspools. But every night after work he would take out his accordion and play old and new songs. And the kids and neighbors would stop by to listen. And I was the proudest kid in the neighborhood." He never forgot that and today as an important executive he takes time out to play, of all things — the harpsichord.

I have been somewhat grieved by the mentality of friends I have who are sincerely trying to live by the Spirit and walk in the Spirit. That is, they are trying to make Jesus Lord of their lives under the guiding light of the Holy Spirit. One of these friends has an excellent talent for scenic painting. I said to her one day,

"What have you been painting lately?"

"Oh nothing," was her reply. "You see I don't have time for that anymore. With all the prayer meetings I go to, and listening to tapes, I have given up painting."

I don't get it. I don't get it at all. I am convinced that whatever talent you have, God wants you to do something with it. And certainly when Jesus becomes Lord of our time He will lead us to find time for it. Not for nothing did he give us the parable of the talents, the gold coins and the three servants, with the focus upon the man who didn't do anything but bury or hide the one coin that was given to him. Jesus said:

> "I tell you that to everyone who has, even more will be given; but the one who does not have, even the little that he has will be taken away from him."
>
> Luke 19, 26.

You say — "That's a hard saying, Lord." And you're right. Jesus always hits it hard when he has to, and on the question of time and talent he's a very hard hitter. If you have and use whatever you have, you will find you will get more. If you don't do anything at all because you excuse yourself by saying you're not much of a much and you don't have anything to work with, you will lose whatever you do have — you will be guilty of abortion of your time and talent. You will be one of those awful persons for whom life has become a yawn and a bore. And since yawning is catchy you will bring some of that yawn and boredom to others. If you keep your light continually under the bushel, you will only have time for the darkness.

You see, Jesus, as Lord of your time, really takes over. He becomes not only Lord of your work time, your spare time, your past-time, but at the same time, Lord of your talents, your energy, your mind, your imagination. And his light within you overcomes the darkness or depression or boredom of your life. You will begin to understand Him when He says:

> "Continue on your way while you have the light, so the darkness will not come upon you. . . ."
>
> John 12, 35.

*lord, jesus, let the light of your holy spirit
shine on every hour
of my day and night
be lord of my time here on this earth
every blessed minute of it.*

*teach me yourself, lord
there's a time for work and a time for play
a time to be noisy, a time to be quiet,
a time for the marketplace and concrete
city
a time for green pastures and still running
waters.
a time for prayer, always time for prayer
and time for doing the everyday things,
the eating and drinking and washing the
car
and feeding the dog and fixing the fence.*

*and less time for talk
and more time for listening.
less time for televiewing
and more time for seeing you
in the smile of a child, the flight of a bird
and the walk of a turtle.*

*lord jesus, be lord of my time here on this
earth
until the time when there is
no time but
the eternity of YOU.*

Chapter 8

JESUS IS LORD!

For me, one of the most blessed and beautiful experiences of the New Pentecost today is to be with my brothers and sisters, Catholics or not, proclaiming the Lordship of Jesus Christ. I have had this experience with small prayer groups, sometimes in a beautiful ranch home of California, sometimes with a little group of God's peasant people in the high Andes. I learned to proclaim Him Lord working for two years in ministry with a Southern Baptist preacher in Peru. I have proclaimed Him Lord with his dear people in the Assembly of God Churches and with the Methodists and the Episcopalians. I have met with thousands who crowded the great churches of Stockholm and Copenhagan to sing, "Jesus is Lord." I have stood in great outdoor prayer meetings in Puerto Rico and Bombay, Mexico and Hawaii with the triumphant echo of "Jesus is Lord" ringing in my ears. This is the great actuality of our day, the fulfillment of the work of the Holy Spirit;

"That at the name of Jesus every knee should bow, in heaven on earth and under the earth, and every tongue confess that Jesus Christ is Lord, to the glory of God the Father."

Philippians 2, 4.

By the grace of God, you and I are called to proclaim the Lordship of Jesus Christ. By the power given to us through the Baptism of the Holy Spirit, God the Father expects it of us, and Jesus Himself with open arms is waiting for us to claim His total embrace as Lord of our lives.

Now unto those to whom much is given, much is expected. You know the Kingdom of God is not only a gift to you, it is a work for you, a task for you; it is a witness you must give.

If you and I are called to proclaim the Lordship of Jesus Christ in our lives, what does this really mean? It's one thing to sing it out beautifully at great prayer meetings and gatherings. It's quite another thing to live in the day-by-day experience of Jesus Lord. And only then do we have the right to say, "Jesus is Lord of my life!"

"Have this mind in yourselves which you have in Christ Jesus, who though He was in the form of God, did not count equality with God a thing to be grasped, but emptied Himself taking the form of a servant." Paul tells us that Jesus, though He was equal to God did not cling to that but emptied Himself and took the form of a servant. And He humbled Himself and became obedient unto death, even to the death on a Cross. And He did all that to serve us, and for love of you and me. Paul says — have the same mind as Jesus.

In proclaiming Jesus, Lord of our lives, we need to ask ourselves, "Are we discovering His mind? Are we thinking His way? Are we asking the Holy Spirit to make Jesus the Lord of all our mind and all our thinking, Lord of all our attitudes towards life and towards people. Claiming the mind of Jesus, making Him the Lord of all our thinking and hoping and desiring, Lord of all our dreams, we come to the point where He leads us to — the emptying of self. You will begin to understand what Jesus said about the grain of wheat: that to bear fruit, it must fall into the ground and die. You will know by experience the paradox of the gospel as He Himself said it:

"Whoever loves his own life will lose it; whoever hates his own life in this world will keep it for life eternal. Whoever wants to serve me must follow me, so that my servant will be with me where I am. My Father will honor him who serves me."

John 12, 25-26.

Now understand that Jesus was not talking about hating our true life. He is the Lord of life and wants us all to love life — every minute of it. Every minute of it is the gift of the Father to us through Jesus. We glorify the Father in His name when we accept the gift of life and try to live it day-by-day, deeply and richly under the Lordship of Jesus.

What Jesus was talking about was hating our selfishness, our pride, our greed to want more, to get ahead of our neighbor, to put ourselves in the number one spot. When you hate your life in that way, you are on your way to keeping your real life for life eternal.

What Jesus is talking about is this. If we want to serve Him and declare Him Lord of our lives, we must follow Him. And following Him means not only up to the Mount of Transfiguration where we can shout with Peter our happy halleluias for the Lord's glory, but it means following Him on the road of Calvary that leads to the Cross. In other words, to enter into the true Lordship of Jesus and make Him Lord of our lives, sooner or later means we arrive at a point of emptiness — emptied of self that we may live in Him and He in us. Paul put it this way:

"So that it is no longer I who live,
but it is Christ who lives in me."
Galatians 2, 20.

This of course is the ultimate. It doesn't happen overnight. It doesn't come about merely by attending prayer meetings or listening to tape recordings of well-known charismatic teachers. That helps. But there is only One who can make it all come true for us — the easy part of it, as well as the hard part of it. And that is Jesus Lord, Himself — through the power of His Holy Spirit.

*lord jesus,
i thank you that life is so very much worth living
when i live with you as my lord —
lord, if there is some area, some place
some dimension
of my life
where you do not yet reign as lord,
forgive me
i know it is my fault, not yours*

*if i still rake over my past,
lord, forgive me, be lord of my past.*

*if i am torn apart, busy and distracted with this present moment
lord, forgive me
be lord of my today*

*if i am nervous about tomorrow,
lord, forgive me
be lord of my future*

*if i am sick with the sickness of mind and body
clinging to habits of sickness
lord, forgive me
be lord of my health, my healing lord.*

*if i hold tight to money and things
knowing my brothers and sisters are
starving and hungry,
lord forgive me, be lord of my treasures.*

*if i am failing to love because my heart is
not right,
lord, forgive me
be lord of my heart, of all my love.*

*if i am wasting my time
letting it slip by, unused, unfruitful
lord, forgive me
be lord of my time*

*yes, lord, i've made a mess of it
most of my life
but now, jesus, lord of my life,
TAKE OVER!*

The first book by George De Prizio, C.S.C. entitled MY GOD, I NEED SOMETHING! is an introduction to Christian Renewal in the Holy Spirit. It is available through CharisPUBLICATIONS at $1.25 per copy.

> Send $2.00 plus 10 per cent shipping charges to:
> CharisPUBLICATIONS,
> P.O. Box 506, La Puente, CA 91747
> California residences must add 6 per cent for sales tax.

CharisTAPES also announces the availability of the following tapes from a recent Prayer Workshop which Father De Prizio conducted in Southern California:

1. The Mystery of Prayer
2. Depth of Charismatic Prayer
3. Prayer Life of Jesus
4. Prayer of Meditation

> Send $3.50 plus 10 per cent shipping charges to:
> CharisTAPES, P.O. Box 506, La Puente, CA 91747
> California residences must add 6 per cent for sales tax.